T0146704

A WIDOW'S MIGHT

A Family Memoir

KATHRYN BOLSER BANKS

A WIDOW'S MIGHT
A FAMILY MEMOIR

iUniverse books may be ordered through booksellers or by contacting:

iUniverse
1663 Liberty Drive
Bloomington, IN 47403
www.iuniverse.com
1-800-Authors (1-800-288-4677)

ISBN: 978-1-5320-0244-1 (sc)
ISBN: 978-1-5320-0245-8 (e)

Library of Congress Control Number: 2016911429

Print information available on the last page.

iUniverse rev. date: 08/04/2016

To Olive Jackson Bolser Hoffman,
my grandmother, and to my beloved grandchildren.
I am honored to provide a link between them.

Lest you forget the things your eyes have seen … make them known to your children and your children's children.
—Deuteronomy 4:9 English Standard Version

Preface

Long before I began the process to publish this book, it was conceived. My natural interest in history was united with intriguing personal stories I heard from my father and grandmother throughout my growing-up years. The past came alive as I learned about their hard times, lessons learned, and "the way it used to be."

Twenty-five years ago, I typed up the stories I had heard for so many years. My grandmother was living then and was able to add details as I requested them. I put the manuscript away with other family memorabilia until my retirement when a longtime family friend and neighbor encouraged me to consider publishing what I had written. She had recently published her memoirs and found it a very satisfying and rewarding experience.

The death of my grandmother occurred soon after the birth of my first grandchild. At that time, I realized that I was a link between generations, a connection that was too valuable to lose. *A Widow's Might* is the result of that realization and the encouragement of a friend.

INTRODUCTION

West Chester, in Southwest Ohio, was a small rural community in 1922, when Olive Naomi Jackson and Joseph Franklin Bolser married. He was the youngest of six sons, and she was reared as an only child after the death of her sister in infancy. Both grew up on farms, and when they married, it was natural that they would work together to establish a dairy herd and build a farming operation of their own. Their family grew as goals were accomplished, but life took some unexpected twists and turns. Perseverance, endurance, and faith played major roles in the survival of their family.

——— CHAPTER 1 ———

CHORES

"Daddy Joe, Daddy Joe, wait for me! Don't you remember? Old Rosie won't come for anybody but me! And you said I could feed Bessie's calf today!"

"Shhh," Joe whispered as he turned to push open the screen door. "Come on, Son, but don't wake your sister and brother. The sun's almost up, and all the cows need to be milked!"

Brownie, the dog, waited on the back porch and joined Joe and Homer as they left the house for the barn. With a lantern in one hand and the shiny clean milk bucket in the other, Joe, along with his two companions, crossed the barnyard in the dim gray light of dawn. Brownie's usual slow, lazy gait had changed to the prance of a frisky pup in the cool freshness of this June morning.

In recent months, five-year-old Homer had become more interested in chores that involved the cows. Joe recognized in his son the same love and understanding of animals that he had possessed since his own boyhood. Milking every morning and evening had become a part of Homer's daily routine. He acted like it was more a privilege than a chore. Joe wasn't sure how long the boy would keep that attitude, because he could recall his own occasional irritations toward the cows with their demands to be milked every twelve hours, 365 days a year.

But those feelings of resentment had been fleeting for Joe. At present, his cows were more than his means of living; they were his pride and joy, especially now with his herd of sixteen registered Holsteins. When he and Olive had married six years before, he had three cows. One was given to him by his father, and one was given to him by her father. The third one he had managed to buy on his own. Now few milking herds in this area could rival Joe Bolser's.

Joe was already a seasoned farmer at age thirty-two. Although he had been required to register with the Selective Service at age twenty-one, his local draft board had never called him to serve during World War I. He was allowed to stay home and work the family farm while his brother Clarence and other friends and relatives had gone off to fight the war. He had grown up farming and continued to practice his trade without interruption during his young adult years.

As Joe opened the door to the dark barn, the sweet smell of hay and grain, mixed with the more pungent odor of the cows, greeted him. The lantern, hanging from a beam in the center of the low-ceilinged milking stable, gave a warm, soft yellow glow. Ruby, the most anxious and demanding of all the cows, bawled to be admitted to the barn. First, Homer and Joe had to scoop just the right amount of grain from the wooden wheelbarrow into each cow's part of the manger. These cows were creatures of habit. They marched to the same stall every morning and every night, content to be chained in, eager to eat the grain and be relieved of the heavy load of milk they carried.

Joe opened the door on the lower end of the barn, and Ruby rushed to take her usual position at the manger. Next was Daisy, the only Jersey cow in the herd, special because of the extra-rich milk she produced. Then came Star, Bessie, Lucky,

Kate, and all the others but Rosie. She always brought up the rear and often needed some coaxing.

"Come on, Rosie," yelled Homer. "Get in here, or I'll give your grain to Bessie!" But she didn't take the next step until Homer walked out the door and across the lot with a sturdy cane in his hand. She moved just in time to avoid a whack across the rump. "Silly cow," murmured Homer. He strutted proudly behind the 1,500-pound cow, driving her toward the door of the barn.

By the time Rosie's long, rough tongue began scraping her grain from the manger, the other cows were nearly finished eating, and Joe had moved the lantern to hang from the beam just behind Bessie's stanchion. Her udder was full and dripping with milk. Joe placed his narrow, wooden milking stool close between Bessie and Kate. Then he squatted on the stool and secured the bucket on the floor between his knees and under the cow. Bessie was one of the nervous ones, often shifting weight from one leg to the other as Joe pulled and squeezed to squirt two warm streams of milk into the bucket. *Ping, ping, ping.* The milk hit the sides of the bucket and rolled down, covering the bottom with white foam.

"When can I milk?" asked Homer.

"Now, you know Bessie's nervous and anxious to get this finished. I'm anxious too. I have three days' work to cram into this one," he added. "Just go find something else to do for now. Maybe you can help me milk Rosie later on."

It was still too dark to hunt for the mama cat's new kittens, and Brownie wasn't in a playful mood. The old dog had curled up to take a nap in a pile of hay. Homer had, on several other mornings, joined Brownie in the extra hay at the end of the manger with the horse blanket pulled over him. It was a good place to snooze because it was next to Rosie, and if he didn't fall asleep too soundly, he could hear Daddy Joe milking her, and he'd ask again to take his turn.

Homer knew he would have plenty to keep him busy after the cows were milked. Cold water would have to be pumped into the trough in the milk house. Four ten-gallon milk cans stood in the trough. Homer's job was to stir the two cans holding this morning's milk to cool it as quickly as possible. These two cans, along with the two filled with last night's milk, would soon be picked up and taken to the dairy. While Homer stirred the warm milk, Joe would open the stable door and release each cow. They always exited the barn so he could clean in preparation for repeating the whole process in twelve short hours.

Chapter 2

More Chores

Olive had heard Homer running through the house at five o'clock this morning. She had been thankful that Fern and Wesley hadn't heard him calling for Joe, and then she dozed off. Olive knew it was time for her to get busy by the light streaming through the window. Joe worked up a big appetite by seven when the milking was done, and he was always anxious to eat and get on with the rest of his chores, especially during the busy spring and summer months. Olive dressed quickly, went downstairs, and fixed a big breakfast for her husband of six years.

Olive had known Joe for many years before they married. She was in the second grade when she met him. She had just changed schools, and the long pretty curls her mother had labored over each morning before school were an irresistible temptation to some of the boys. They were relentless, pulling her curls at every chance. The day she cried was the day one of the big boys made the others leave her alone. That big boy was Joe Bolser, and he had won a special place in her heart.

Several years after that incident, Olive received another hint that she was special to Joe. The annual church ice cream social was one of the social highlights of the year. He had asked to walk her home. She yearned to say yes, but she had to explain, "Mother will say I'm too young. I know she will."

"How old are you?" he had asked.

When Olive replied that she was fourteen, Joe laughed and said, "Your mother is right, but I'll be around later." And he was. Two years later, in alliance with her father, Olive persuaded her mother to allow her to have her first date.

Olive and Joe dated for two more years until she graduated from high school. At that time—June 1921—the most crucial decision of her eighteen years had to be made. Olive's father offered to send her to college with her best friend. After one year there, she could become a teacher. Or she could have a wedding. A family or a career? No woman was allowed both. Which would it be? Her decision had not taken long. One year after graduation, on June 7, 1922, she and Joe married.

Olive's parents provided a beautiful wedding for their only child. Vows were exchanged in the parlor of the family home under a large white bell. Olive's mother, a talented seamstress, fashioned her gown from white satin and lace. Her veil was dress length, she carried white roses, and the bridesmaid wore pink.

On that June evening, the guests were enjoying ice cream and cake when the yard filled with neighbors and acquaintances for an old-fashioned serenade. They yelled, rang cowbells, and shot shotguns into the air. The noise continued until she and Joe appeared outside and Joe passed around the customary wooden buckets of candy. It was a wonderful celebration.

Now six years later as a wife and mother, she woke to face the demands of this busy Monday morning. Her children, ages five, four, and two, left Olive little time for herself, especially on wash day! Even before going to the little brick smokehouse to get bacon, she pulled the large copper boiler from its corner.

After the bacon and eggs were fried, the water had to be carried from outside and dumped into the boiler to heat on the range.

The range was always hot and ready for the frying pan each morning when Olive entered the kitchen. Joe's first job every day was to toss a few corncobs soaked in coal oil under some kindling in the range. The corncobs never failed to make the wood burn into a hot fire in time to cook breakfast.

Olive had time to empty one bucket of wash water into the boiler before Joe came in with his milk bucket and a special crock full of Daisy's milk. The thick cream had already started rising to the top and would be churned into butter. Daisy's cream was so thick there was always plenty of butter—and even extra to sell to Fred DeBord at the grocery store. He paid twenty-five cents for every one-pound roll of butter Olive brought to him.

Once the milk was separated from the cream, they drank it or poured it over their Post Toasties, that new, dry, ready-to-eat cereal that Fred had recently placed on his store shelves. If any milk was left, Olive usually made cottage cheese. After allowing the skimmed milk to sour on the back of the range, she would pour the soured milk into one of the muslin sacks that sugar came in and then hang it on the clothesline for a couple of days to curdle. Adding a little cream would finish the process and get it ready for the dinner table.

As Homer and Joe washed their hands in the basin in the corner of the kitchen, Olive filled three plates with eggs and bacon. Joe reviewed his plans for the rest of the day. "I'll be going to the back field soon after breakfast," he told her almost apologetically. Olive liked to have him close by on wash day. Although the gasoline-powered wringer washer was a big improvement over the washboard of a few years ago, the motor that sat to the side of the wooden tub was temperamental and often needed his attention.

"I still have some corn to plant, and this weather may not hold out much longer," he explained.

"Better take advantage of the sunshine, but if you don't have a big dinner waiting on you at noon, you'll know that the washer and I have been at odds," she warned.

"I'm going with you, Daddy," Homer said.

"You'd better ask your mother, and you'd better be willing to stay out there awhile. I'm not coming back until dinnertime, and it's too far for you to walk alone," replied Joe.

"Can I, Mother? Please?"

"It's all right with me. I surely don't need all of you children under my feet when I'm dipping hot water from the boiler and carrying it to the washer. But after dinner, you're going to rest. Getting up at five o'clock to milk is a little early for a fellow your age!"

"All right," answered Homer with an agreeable grin.

"Well, come on then." Joe swallowed his last bite of breakfast and crossed the floor to get his hat hanging near the door. "The sooner we get the rest of our chores done, the sooner we'll get to the corn planting."

CHAPTER 3

BARN AND FIELD

"I get to feed Bessie's calf," Homer yelled as he ran out the door to catch up with Joe.

"I know. But first you'll pump water for the horses while I get their feed." Only the cows received as much care and attention as Ned, Bill, Jeff, and Jim, the team of workhorses. They worked hard and were well paid in fresh water, corn, oats, and hay.

The routine chores, repeated twice a day every day, took little time. As soon as the horse trough had been filled with water, Homer ran to the milking stable to grab the bucket with the milk that Joe reserved for Bessie's little heifer calf. Bessie nursed her calf for three weeks, and just last Wednesday, they were separated. Both cow and calf had bawled for each other that first day, but by now, they seemed to have forgotten that the other existed. The calf wasn't eating as much grain as she should be, though, and she needed to get a little more milk to supplement her new diet. The calf didn't catch on right away. Drinking from a bucket was different from drinking from her mother. But a few downward pushes on the calf's head with Joe's hand had helped the calf get a taste of the milk. Homer learned to hold tight once the calf started drinking. She often rammed the bottom of the bucket with her head, lifting it into the air and spilling the milk all over anyone who happened to be near. In a matter of seconds, the milk was gone, and Homer hopped quickly over the gate. Hungry calves tried to eat everything, and their tongues were slobbery wet and sandpaper rough!

Meanwhile, Joe fed the hogs and carried several buckets of water to the trough in the pigpens. That finished the morning chores, so Joe led the horses outside to be harnessed and hitched to the corn planter. Ned and Bill would handle the planter this morning. Jim and Jeff would finish what was left after dinner. The more difficult jobs of plowing, dragging, and disking, which required all four horses, had been finished early in the spring. They had earned some time off now.

The planter was filled with big, promising kernels of corn. Last winter, Joe spent several days looking for the best ears of corn in the corncrib. He then shelled that corn from the cob to be stored until planting time. Even the small or slightly deformed kernels at either end of these exceptional ears of corn were thrown out for the chickens. Only the best kernels of the best ears were saved for planting. Now, with two bushels of seed corn left and only seven acres to plant, Joe knew he would have seed to spare.

The seat of the corn planter, designed to hold one person, had proven itself strong enough to support a large man and his little boy on several other occasions and was put to the test one more time as Homer hopped onto his daddy's knee. "Giddyap!" commanded Joe as he held the reins loosely, and they were off to the back field.

With well-trained horses and a planter adjusted to drop the seeds at just the right time, Joe relaxed as he rode down a long row behind Ned and Bill. An occasional command of "gee" or "haw" was all that was necessary to keep the horses on track.

Homer rode for a while, but after two trips up and down the field, he decided to get off at the end of the row. Brownie watched from under a clump of trees on the edge of the nearby pasture. It looked inviting to Homer, a place to cool off and pick up sticks. He passed over the sticks that were dry and brittle as well as the most pliable green ones in favor of the sticks that were just right to cut into little pieces or to whittle. This back field provided an abundant supply of sticks, and it was also far away from the house and Mother's watchful eyes!

Homer carefully pulled his prized, blue-handled penknife from his pocket. Mother had complained about the penknife from the day Homer and his daddy had brought it home from DeBord's store. "He's too little for that," she warned. And then when he cut himself on the hand one day, she really got riled. But Homer and Daddy Joe convinced her that the cut was minor and he would be more careful from now on.

Whittle, whittle, cut, cut. Scrape, scrape, cut. Oops! A little slip, and the knife slid right into the end of his thumb. Homer worried more about what Mother would say than he did about the sting of the cut. He ran quickly to the spring at the edge of the clump of trees. The cool water helped stop the bleeding, but before Homer could get back to his sticks, Joe and the horses headed toward him.

Joe never let his horses get too thirsty. He had been glad to find this spring at the back of the farm. It provided cool refreshment for both him and his horses without taking time to go all the way back to the barns.

"Homer, what are you doing?" Joe asked as soon as he stopped the horses.

"Nothing," Homer replied.

"Let me see that hand you just jerked out of the water." Joe raised his eyebrows and shook his head. He pulled a clean handkerchief from his overalls pocket and wrapped it around the cut. "That will keep it clean until we get ready to go back to the house," he said, and he turned the horses from the spring. "Now be careful!" he called as he headed back to his work.

CHAPTER 4

CAUGHT NAPPING

Dinner was on the table, and clean clothes were on the clothesline when Homer and Joe got back to the house at noon.

"Looks like we've both made headway this morning," Joe said as he took off his hat and poured water in the basin to wash his hands and face. "I'll be able to finish that field before milking time. Is the washing machine working for you, Olive?"

She was scraping mashed potatoes from the pan on the range. "The *washing machine* is not the problem," she answered.

"How have you two been?" he asked, pulling Fern to his lap as he sat down. Wesley sat in the high chair beside Joe's place at the table.

"I'll answer that!" offered Olive.

"I've been good, Daddy," Fern interrupted. "I played with Mother's muffin tin and cake pans and my dolly all day,"

"Then it must be you," Joe said as he gazed into the innocent eyes of his younger son. Wesley had a way of finding mischief since he grew bored quickly with such things as spoons, pots, and pans. Being underfoot on wash day was especially dangerous with hot water being dipped and carried from the boiler on the range to the washtub in the summer kitchen. He usually had to be caged in the old playpen that one of Joe's older brothers had built when his children were babies.

"Today," Olive explained, "he managed to get out of the playpen. He found the one slat that was loose and kicked and pushed until he moved it. That left a hole just big enough to squeeze through. He had gotten really good at it by the time I started rinsing the first load of clothes. He should be ready to take a long nap this afternoon while I finish my washing. And that reminds me," she said looking at Homer, "you have to take a nap this afternoon too. I think you must be tired. You haven't said anything since you and Daddy came in. Are you all right?"

"I'm fine," Homer answered, keeping his thumb carefully curled out of sight as he finished his meat and potatoes.

"Well, there's nothing wrong with your appetite," remarked Olive. "But you're bound to be sleepy getting up at five in the morning! By the time I get these dishes cleared off the table, I want you lying down."

Homer didn't argue. "First, though," he said, "I'd better check on Brownie's water."

As the door slammed behind Joe and Homer, Wesley blinked heavily. Olive washed the food from his hands and face and whisked him upstairs to his crib. *I'll at least be able to wash the overalls in peace*, she thought as she returned to the empty kitchen.

Olive washed the dishes and checked the temperature of the wash water heating on the range.

"Fern, have you seen Homer?" she called out through the screen door.

"He went around the back of the house with Brownie." Fern didn't lift her eyes from the "grass muffins" she was fixing in one of the old muffin tins.

"Homer!" Olive called as she walked around the house. Then she saw Brownie, his front end inside the doghouse and his back end sticking out. "You're a silly old dog, Brownie!" She laughed as she reached down to pet him. That roused Brownie, and he backed out of the house. Olive caught a glimpse of a shoe. Peering into the dark doghouse, she saw that the shoe was Homer's. "Are you trying to hide in there?" she asked. As her eyes adjusted, she could see Homer napping in the doghouse. She grabbed his arm and pulled. With some effort, she pried him out.

"When I told you to lie down, I had a couch or even a rug on the floor in mind," she chuckled. "Now let's get into our house and find a better place for a nap than the doghouse. Let's go."

Homer took her hand, shuffled drowsily into the living room, and plopped onto the couch. He fell asleep before Olive was able to get his shoes off.

Her eyes caught a glimpse of Homer's hand dangling off the couch near the floor where she set his shoes. "Another cut! That knife has to go!" she muttered aloud. Homer didn't hear or respond, so she slid her hand carefully into his pocket, gently grasped the knife between two fingers, and pulled it out. She quickly poked it into the pocket of her apron and returned to the kitchen and her washer.

CHAPTER 5

PICTURE DAY

"Play peekaboo. Sometimes that works," Olive said.

"But I might get dirty or mess up my hair. You told me to stay pretty," Fern replied. "Besides, I think he's mad. Peekaboo won't help when he gets mad."

"Hurry, Homer! Get those clothes on by yourself so I can get Wesley dressed." Olive wondered if this portrait was going to be worth all the trouble. "Come on," Olive said as she reached for Wesley in the playpen. "Let's get you washed off and your clothes changed. Then we'll be ready to go."

Wesley laughed and jabbered with glee at being set free from the playpen, but he squirmed and fussed during the washing and dressing procedures.

"These shoes are too little," Homer said. "I don't think I can go."

"Squeeze your feet in. You won't have to wear them all day! Besides, those shoes can't be too little. We always buy your good shoes big. They're just not broken in yet."

"But I wanted to go with Daddy to the back field to plow corn!"

"You can go with your daddy tomorrow or the next day," Olive said. "We couldn't go to the photographer on Monday or

Tuesday. Too many clothes to wash, iron, and mend! Tomorrow I have to churn butter and pick the beans in the garden. Friday's always cleaning day. It has to be today!"

"Why?" Homer asked.

"I just explained!"

"But why do we have to have a picture made at all?" Homer said.

"Because everybody has a picture made. Don't they, Mother? Grandma said so! That's why she made me this pretty dress. I love it!" Fern whirled around in a happy dance.

"Come on! Everybody in the automobile." Olive gave herself a glimpse in the mirror and a quick stroke with the hairbrush.

The black Model T sedan was parked in the barnyard. Unlike most of the women around here, Olive was completely at ease with an automobile. Her father had bought his Model T in 1918 when she was fifteen years old, just five years after Henry Ford had introduced the assembly line for his popular automobile. She had been given the free driving lessons and had proved to be a very quick and eager learner.

Fern and Homer climbed into the back as Olive set Wesley in the front seat. Under the steering wheel, she felt for the spark lever. She pulled the lever up before going around to the front of the car to crank it. Forgetting to do so could cause the crank to kick and result in a broken arm.

Cold weather made starting the car a real challenge, but in the warmth of this summer day, it started after just a few turns of the crank. Olive quickly hopped into the driver's seat, adjusted the spark and gas levers, and pushed the pedal on the left to the floor. This put the car in low gear, and they were off, circling the barnyard to the narrow gravel road that led to Hamilton and the photographer. Olive released the pedal and adjusted the gas. They traveled at speeds up to thirty miles an hour before they met another car. Then, putting the left pedal back into the neutral position and tapping the brake pedal on the right, Olive was able to slow down and pull toward the side of the road. The middle pedal was only used for backing up.

While Olive drove, Fern sang a little song, Wesley dozed, and Homer waved to farmers working in the fields.

CHAPTER 6

SATURDAY

Coffee cake! Homer could recognize that smell a mile away. It was the only thing that could lure him away from Daddy Joe and the horses as they got drinks in the barnyard before returning to the field to cut more hay. The smell of coffee cake promised more than good things to eat. It meant this was baking day, and baking day was also grocery day. A trip to the grocery often led to a little longer trip into town and to the movie theater.

"I smell coffee cakes," Homer announced as the screen door slammed behind him.

"So that's what brings you in here." Olive laughed. "They won't be done for a while, and I don't want you to ruin your dinner. Just don't get in a big hurry to eat any."

"Are we going to the store and the movie tonight?" Homer's his mind raced past the coffee cakes to other possibilities for this day.

"Yes, if your daddy gets the hay mowed in good time. If he doesn't start the milking on schedule, we won't be able to go to the movie, though."

"Yeah!" Homer darted back out the door. Saturday, in addition to all the enjoyable activities, brought baths and clean clothes. Homer wanted to find better things to do right now, and he wanted to avoid bath time as long as possible.

With the promise of excitement and fun later on, the rest of the morning dragged for Homer. Daddy Joe was cutting hay in the field next to the house, so there was nothing new to explore there. His penknife had been gone now for weeks. He continued to search, and he was running out of new places to look. Brownie was taking a nap, and Fern was busy concocting a new kind of "muffin."

Kicking a cloud of dust as he walked, Homer crossed the barnyard to take a stroll through the barn. He visited the new calf recently separated from its mother, but Homer could endure its rough tongue only a few minutes. As he escaped from the reach of the calf, he caught a glimpse of the wild kittens that had been in hiding until just a few days ago. Trying to coax the kittens out from under the horse manger brought nothing but spats and hisses. Homer knew from experience that reaching for an unfriendly kitten could be very painful. So he left them alone.

The rooster that sometimes chased Homer and Fern sauntered through the barn, and Homer eased back into a dark corner. He let the aggressive rooster pass, and then he looked under the corncrib. There were likely to be some eggs there that would make a good surprise for Mother when he went in to eat.

It must be about dinnertime, he thought. *I hear Daddy and the horses coming this way.* Homer hurried across the barnyard to look under the corncrib. He carefully picked up three eggs and placed them, one at a time, in a bucket. Slowly and carefully, he started for the house while Joe watered and unhitched the team.

"Oh, for me?" gasped Olive as she peered into the bucket. "Where did you find these? I just gathered eggs a few hours ago."

"Under the corncrib," replied Homer proudly.

"You know where the hens like to lay their eggs, don't you? It's so warm that I think you'd better put them down in the spring cellar. And you'd better do it right away. If Wesley gets them, they'll be scrambled before their time!"

Homer opened the door to the steps that led to the part of the cellar where a spring trickled all year long. In the hot days of summer, it held a good supply of butter, eggs, and milk. When Homer got back to the kitchen, Joe had washed up and Wesley and Fern were in their chairs. Time to eat a special meal. Only on Saturdays were there loaves of bread fresh from the oven and coffee cakes for dessert!

CHAPTER 7

TO TOWN

The rest of Saturday passed quickly. Joe finished cutting the hay early in the afternoon and left it to dry in the sun for two or three days. The next step would be raking it into windrows, gathering it onto the wagons, hauling it into the barn, and storing it for the long winter.

For now, the hay could be forgotten, and other things could be accomplished. First was provision for a tasty Sunday dinner. He caught, killed, and plucked a plump young rooster and took it to Olive in the kitchen. She soaked the chicken in cold water and set it in the spring cellar until it was time to fry it the next day.

Joe offered to take Wesley outside to sit under the shade tree with him for a few minutes. "If you can get some food together for a quick supper while I get myself a drink of water and cool off for a while, I'll be able to start the milking early. Then we can stop at the grocery and get to Mason in plenty of time for the movie," Joe said.

"That's a deal!" Olive quickly gathered up leftovers from the noon meal to put on the table. In practically no time, supper was finished, the table was cleared, and the bathwater was heating on the range. While Joe did the milking, Olive gave herself and the three children a bath from the basin in the kitchen. Everyone had a complete change of clothes on Saturday, always leaving a large pile of dirty laundry for wash day.

Olive managed to keep the children amused and clean while Joe took a bath and changed into clean clothes. As Joe put on his shoes, Olive herded the three children to the automobile.

"Oh, I forgot my butter and eggs," Olive muttered as Joe approached the Model T. "I'll be right back," she called as she ran to the spring cellar. By the time Joe had cranked the engine and plopped into the driver's seat, she had returned with the roll of creamy butter and six dozen eggs.

A few minutes later, they were in Maud, a crossroad with DeBord's Store and a couple of houses. Fred DeBord was a bachelor who had migrated from Kentucky as a teenager to take a job as a stock boy in Cincinnati. After traveling a little farther north, he established a store of his own. Keeping it well stocked and treating his regular customers like family, he had made his grocery a success.

Fred stocked all the staples like flour, sugar, and salt. Thick, round crackers were kept in big, open barrels, and coffee was ground right in the store. Coal oil and cleaning products were available too. Fred kept up with all the latest trends. Olive had purchased a mop there recently, a new invention to help keep women from spending so much time on their hands and knees. It was such a simple idea that had quickly gained popularity.

Olive's grocery list was short tonight. With fresh fruits and vegetables plentiful in her orchard and garden, there was no need to buy many White Villa cans at this time of year. She did buy sugar for canning her fruit and some more Ivory soap for bathing. She had made plenty of lye soap this spring with the old lard from last fall's butchering, but that was only for laundry. Even the toughest skin couldn't withstand the constant use of lye soap.

With such a short grocery list and some extra money from the sale of her eggs and butter, Olive was able to buy some dried peaches and apricots that Fred had recently stocked. They were a real treat!

The children always headed straight for the candy counter. Daddy Joe was a soft touch, and Fred always managed to miscount, dropping a few extra pieces into each of their bags. "Give me one of those and one of those and three of these." Fern stood on her tiptoes and pointed to her favorite candies through the glass case that enclosed the sweet assortment.

"You folks going to the movie this evening?" Fred asked as he boxed the groceries.

"That's right, Fred. Get somebody to close for you tonight and come with us," Joe said.

"Oh, I'd better not," he answered. "What's showing?"

"Laurel and Hardy tonight. We saw a good western last week. You really ought to come with us sometime," Olive added.

"Maybe I will. But you better get those youngsters loaded up or you'll miss the show yourselves," Fred replied.

"See you next week, Fred."

"Take care."

A line was forming at the movie theater as Joe parked the car. The theater was almost always full for its weekly movie. Mr. Bingham, the owner, ran a garage in the other half of the building during the rest of the week. On Saturdays, he closed the garage and opened his theater.

A dollar admitted Joe's entire family. Fern, Homer, and Wesley were happy to watch the movie and listen to the pianist.

The picture on the screen and the music from the piano told the story. The script printed below the picture, while helpful to the adults, was really not important to the children. Munching on their penny candy, watching the movie, and then dozing off to sleep was their normal Saturday-night routine.

CHAPTER 8

FAITH, FOOD, AND FUN

"You two make a fine-looking pair in the Sunday clothes Grandma made you! It's no wonder she enjoys taking you to Sunday school with her." Homer's long stockings, knickers, and matching jacket were a fine complement to Fern's frilly white stockings and blonde slippers.

"You know, I was your age, Homer, when I spoke my first piece at church. It was a long, three-stanza poem. Quite a challenge for a five-year-old. But your grandma drilled me and drilled me. I repeated it perfectly too—except for the last line. I forgot it, so I went and took my seat. As soon as I sat down, I remembered it. I jumped up, ran to the front of the church, and finished my piece. I couldn't figure out why everyone laughed!"

"Will they make me say a piece if I go to Sunday school?" Homer asked nervously.

"No," Olive said. "I know you're not ready for that yet. Maybe you or Fern can say one on Rally Day this fall."

Homer still looked a little worried as Fern screamed from the kitchen, "They're here! Come on, Homer!"

"Good-bye and behave yourselves," Olive said. "I'll have the chicken fried by the time you get home." Olive's mind remained on the memories of her churchgoing days as she retrieved the frying chicken from the spring cellar and put the big black cast-iron skillet on the range. Her strict Methodist parents had taken her to church every Sunday when she was a child. Only after Olive had married and begun to have children of her own had she missed any Sunday services. Since no respectable woman allowed herself to be seen in public places when pregnant, Olive had little chance to attend church in the last five years. With her children so close together, she had been confined to her home, preparing to have a child or taking care of a baby. Perhaps soon, when Wesley got just a little older, she and Joe could get back to the Sunday-morning services. Until then, she would continue to keep in touch with her longtime church friends at the Women's Society of Christian Service meetings held once a month on Wednesday afternoons at the homes of the members.

Olive's sharp knife cut through the plump, meaty rooster. She and her family had eaten fried chicken many Sundays at her grandma's table. Along with creamy mashed potatoes and smooth tapioca pudding, the crispy fried chicken had been a treat that automatically followed the morning services every Sunday.

Unlike Olive and her family, Joe had never been an every-Sunday churchgoer. Some of his leisure activities were on his in-laws' list of forbidden behaviors. Dancing, card playing, and Sunday-afternoon ballgames were considered forms of transgression, but his large, muscular frame, keen interest, and natural talent blended to make him a much sought-after player by the various baseball teams in the area. In his younger days, he had been approached by a scout for the Cincinnati Reds professional ball club. His ankles were weak, though, and his running ability was limited. So he didn't get past the first step with the Reds. But even now, in his thirties, he continued to play in a community league. He had been shocked at the beginning of the season when a team from a town several miles away offered to pay him five dollars a game to be their catcher.

Almost every Sunday afternoon during the summer, Joe sweated on a baseball field instead of the hay, wheat, and cornfields where he worked the other six days of the week. The ball field offered release from the farm, its routine chores, its monotony, and its worries. With an extra five dollars in his pocket, he went home every Sunday evening to his ever-recurring job of milking hot and tired, but relaxed. He savored every long hit and extraordinary play he had made that day.

CHAPTER 9

THRESHING RING

It felt strange to sit at the kitchen table and just let her thoughts wander. Midmorning was usually such a busy time for Olive, but this morning was different. Joe had left almost three hours earlier, chewing his last bite of bacon just as he had the past two days of this week and four days last week. Today, he left with a prediction and a warning. He said that he would probably be home earlier and that she should be prepared.

Each time the phone rang, Olive had started toward it before waiting to listen for the four rings that signaled a call for her. The first call to come over their party line was one ring. Margaret Peters called every morning to check on her elderly aunt, Mrs. Gray. The next call, just a few minutes ago, had been three rings for the Joneses on down the road.

Now with the cherry cobbler baked and cooling on the counter, Olive was unsure about what to do next.

Ring! Ring! Ring! Ring!

That's it, Olive thought as she crossed the kitchen to pick up the receiver. "Hello," she blurted into the wooden box on the wall.

"Olive, this is Helen. They're heading for your place. The first team and wagon ought to be there soon. The threshing machine's starting down our lane now."

"I've been waiting. Joe said that he thought they'd be here for dinner, and I was afraid to start doing anything else until I found out if I'd be feeding an army of men today or not!"

"I'll be over to help you with the food," Helen said. "Could you use a couple of cherry pies?"

"Sure could! I'm not sure the cobbler I fixed will stretch far enough. Thanks for the pies and the phone call. I've just been waiting, not knowing what I should be doing. Now I have my work cut out for me!"

Olive pushed down on the hook that held the receiver. She then released it and quickly turned the crank on the side of the phone. "Edna, this is Olive. Ring my mom for me please. That's right—4212." She waited a long minute. Then she heard her mother's voice. "Mom, they're coming! The whole threshing crew will be here for dinner. See you in a little while."

"Homer! Fern!" Olive called as she stood in front of the pantry, locating the cans of salmon she had bought on her last trip to DeBord's. "Here," she barked as she handed two cans to each child. "Put these on the table and then go out to the shed and get the old washtub. I think if you help each other, you can drag it over to the pump. Then start filling it with water. Those men will be hot and dirty when they get ready to eat!"

"What men?" Fern asked.

"The threshers. They're finally coming here, aren't they?" Homer exclaimed. Joe had promised Homer that after he helped his neighbors thresh their wheat, they would all come to help thresh his. "Can I go down by the road and watch for them? I think I hear the threshing machine now!"

"Put those cans on the table, help your sister with the washtub, and then you can go watch for the threshing ring.

But you come back up here later and run some water in the tub. I expect you'll be doing a lot of pumping all afternoon. This crew has a water boy, but I know he'll need some help on a hot day like today."

"Yippee!" Homer nearly bounced the cans onto the top of the table and darted for the door. "Hurry, Fern! Don't be so pokey!"

"Wait a minute," Fern said. "Is Grandma coming to help?"

"Yes, she'll be here soon."

"Good! Grandma can help us fix the food and watch Wesley. I'll be back in when Grandma gets here," she said, and off she skipped.

Yes, thought Olive. *Wesley won't be content to stay in that playpen much longer, and I have to get these potatoes peeled and the salmon loaves in the oven.*

The threshing machine chugged along as the caravan of wagons rattled along behind it. The horses, all recently shod in preparation for the trips over the rough gravel roads, shuffled along in front of each wagon. Joe, driving his team, led the procession, which was greeted and then escorted up the lane by a jubilant boy and an excited girl. The wagons headed straight for the lower wheat field. Only the last wagon, which carried a little cart and several water jugs, stopped at the house. The water boy and his dad quickly unloaded them, and then the last wagon joined the others already in the field.

The experienced teams of workhorses knew exactly what to do. Once the driver started them, the horses needed no further guidance. They tromped in a straight line between the rows of wheat shocks at a slow, steady pace, stopping only at the end of the field or at the command of "Whoa" if some trouble required a little extra time. Thus the driver was free to place the shocks of wheat in just the right position on the wagon as men walking along on both sides hurled them up to him.

"Daddy Joe!" Homer called as Joe's team approached the end of the second row. "Come get a drink. I pumped and pumped to fill all these jugs. Aren't you thirsty?"

Joe jumped off the wagon and signaled for his two hired hands to come get a drink. "That water does look good. It's getting hotter out here by the minute. Does your mother have dinner ready yet?"

"Oh, yeah," Homer said. "I'm supposed to tell you to come in and wash up now. The food's ready to eat."

"Did you see the threshing machine yet?" Joe asked Homer.

"Yes! I saw it!"

"I told you it was something to see! Just wait till we feed it some wheat shocks after dinner. You'll see a mountain of straw form on one side while all the little grains of wheat are dumped out on the other side, separated and ready to use in no time! You go tell the others it's time to eat. We'll load just a few more shocks on our wagon. Then we'll be ready for dinner, and we'll bring a full wagon in with us. Get some feed and water ready for the horses. They're hungry and thirsty too!"

Chapter 10

Sickness

Something's really wrong, Olive thought. The jangle of the harness and snorting of the horses told her that Joe and the team were back from the field. She knew that nothing but serious trouble would bring him back a mere half hour after he had harnessed the horses to the wheat drill and set off for the field. *I knew when Homer got up before Joe and came into our bedroom to get him that Joe must have been awfully tired. He seemed almost normal after breakfast, though. I just hoped …*

"Mother! Mother!" Homer yelled, interrupting her thoughts and sending her out the screen door on a run.

"What's wrong?"

"You're going to have to put the team away. I've got to get to bed," Joe wheezed as he dropped the reins and stumbled toward the house.

"Homer and Fern, you see what you can do to help your daddy while I put the team away. Go on! I'll be inside in a minute."

Her experience as a girl with workhorses on her father's farm allowed Olive to manage the team and the harness with little trouble. The job was accomplished quickly and mechanically because Olive's mind was on Joe as it had been for several weeks.

He had been sick for a week when she first took him to the doctor, and the diagnosis had been the grippe. The stomach distress and fever seemed to run its course, but Joe failed to regain his strength and energy. Now he seemed to be worse than ever.

Olive raced back to the house to find Fern and Homer entertaining Wesley, whom she had left in the playpen. "Where's your daddy?" she demanded.

"Upstairs," answered Fern. "Wesley wanted Daddy, but he told us to play with Wesley. I think he's sick again."

"You're doing a good job of babysitting. Keep it up while I check on your daddy." She climbed the stairs and turned into the room to find Joe in bed.

"You're getting worse, aren't you?" Olive's voice quivered slightly as she laid her hand on his forehead.

"Yes," he moaned. "You're going to have to make some arrangements."

"I know," Olive replied. "I'll call the doctor right away. Another doctor. The one you saw before was wrong. You are sicker than he thinks. This isn't the grippe."

"No, I mean some arrangements for the milking and the field work. I can't do it. I just can't do it," he whispered.

"Yes, that too. Don't worry." She tried to cover the concern in her voice. "You just rest."

Olive stood close by as he dozed off, and then she busied herself turning the bedroom into a sickroom, pulling the curtains, filling a glass and basin with water, and getting the slop bucket that she kept handy for the children and their middle-of-the-night emergencies. She knew that Joe would be unable to travel outside to either the outhouse or the water pump.

Checking on the children, Olive found that Wesley had managed to escape from the playpen, but he was being entertained and guarded from harm by the two older children. They seemed to understand that she was busy with other very important matters.

The first concern was tonight's milking. Olive grabbed the telephone receiver from its hook and rang for the operator. She gave her the number of Hap Walters, an older man who Joe had hired several times before when he needed help.

"Hap," Olive called into the phone when he answered, "I'm going to need some help. Joe's gotten awfully sick. Can you milk tonight and the next couple days?"

Olive was relieved to hear his answer. "I'm glad to know that," she told him. "See you over here about five thirty."

She pushed down on the hook, released it, and cranked the handle on the side of the phone once again. "Edna," she called to the operator, "give me 4212, please." "Mom," she said when she heard her mother's voice, "Joe's gotten a lot worse. I'm going to call another doctor. I don't know what he'll say. I might need some help with the children." Olive felt her throat tightening as she quickly reviewed the events of the morning. She felt some relief, though, as her mother promised to stay close to the phone and come when she was needed.

The last call was to Dr. Williams. Friends and neighbors had spoken of him with high regard. *Maybe*, she thought, *he can help us now.*

CHAPTER 11

WORRY AND WORK

Olive watched intently as Dr. Williams examined Joe. It seemed to her that she had waited an eternity for him to come. To Olive's relief, yesterday's phone call to Dr. Williams had resulted in a promise to come this morning. But twenty-four hours of watching Joe lie in weakness and discomfort, not knowing what to expect, had made it a difficult wait.

"Come with me, Mrs. Bolser," he whispered as he left the room. "You mentioned before we came upstairs that you believed he has been hemorrhaging?"

"Yes, earlier when I took the slop bucket out …"

"You found blood," he said, finishing the sentence for her.

"Yes. What do you think it is, Doctor?"

"I'm almost sure it's typhoid fever. Where do you get your drinking water?"

"Well, we have a pump in the yard right outside the back door. And, of course, Joe and the animals drink from springs in the field. Then we have a spring in back of the barn too."

Dr. Williams turned to go down the steps. Olive followed him to the kitchen.

"I'm going to send some men out from the board of health to test the water. I suggest that you get your drinking water somewhere else for now."

"What about Joe?"

"Mrs. Bolser, he's a very sick man. I think you know that." Olive nodded as she felt her heart jump into her throat. She strained to catch every word and gesture the doctor made. "I want to admit him to the hospital," the doctor added. Olive nodded again, now more convinced than ever that Joe's condition was serious. "Mercy is a fine new hospital. I'll make the arrangements there. Do you know of an ambulance service that can transport him?"

"Yes, I'll contact them," she responded.

"Tell them to bring him this afternoon. Call my office if you have any problems with the arrangements. I'll send someone from the board of health out tomorrow, and I'll see you at the hospital later this afternoon."

Trying to comprehend all that the doctor had told her, Olive was lost in her thoughts for several seconds before she was aware of Homer tugging at her arm.

"What did the doctor say? Is Daddy Joe going to be all right?" he asked.

"Your daddy's really sick. The doctor is going to put him in the hospital," Olive said.

"What's that?"

"It's a place where very, very sick people go because the best doctors and nurses work there. They'll give Daddy medicine and care that we can't give him here at home."

"How long will he have to stay? Is Hap going to do the milking again? I don't think Daddy would like the way he does it."

"I don't know how long he'll be there, but you stay out of Hap's way. We need him right now," Olive said. "Now go get Fern and Wesley. Tell them to come out here to the kitchen."

CHAPTER 12

ANXIOUS DAYS

"Do you have to go back to the hospital again? When are you and Daddy going to come home?" Fern whined as she sat on Olive's lap.

"I can't answer that. Daddy's still awfully sick. I like to come home, though, especially when I see you and Wesley so healthy. The doctor's medicine and the shots helped you two."

"They're doing just fine, now," Olive's mother said. "No need to worry about them."

"And it looks as if Homer and I have escaped it completely. I'm thankful for that too. It's hard to figure how the biggest, strongest one of us all is the one who just can't conquer this typhoid. Now come here, Wesley," Olive called.

He ran across the kitchen floor and pushed Fern to make room on his mother's lap.

"Hop-hopital," he stuttered. The word had become part of his vocabulary after four weeks of hearing it discussed over and over.

"Yes," Olive answered as she hugged them both. "You be good for your grandma. I'm getting good reports about Homer while he's been with Uncle Sam and Aunt Marie. So you two behave too. I'll be back to see you tomorrow or the next day."

"I suppose you'll be staying at Oney's again tonight. You do need your rest," Olive's mother reminded her.

"Yes, it works out well having Joe's brother right there in Hamilton. But I'm going back to the hospital first. One more hug, and then I have to go," she said to Fern and Wesley. "See you tomorrow."

The mixture of bright sunshine and cool temperatures on a colorful fall day with the good condition of everyone at home lifted Olive's spirits as she made the familiar trip back to the hospital. Maybe the nurse would finally greet her with good news instead of the usual discouraging report of high fever, weight loss, and lack of response to the medicine.

Meeting several more cars than usual, Olive wondered for a moment what might be the reason for the traffic. *Oh, this is fair week. Everyone is heading home to do evening chores after a day at the county fair.*

Those four days in late October when the county fair took place had always been special to Olive. As a little girl, she had traveled with her parents by horse and buggy to see the sights and socialize with other fair-goers. A picnic lunch followed by cotton candy, ice cream, candy, popcorn, or waffles had become a tradition. She could always count on riding both rides there: the Ferris wheel and the merry-go-round. Her mother always spent much time inspecting handiwork in the art hall, and her dad enjoyed the poultry and horses on display.

The livestock exhibits had grown since those days, and there were rumors of a cattle show being organized. Just for a moment, Olive allowed herself to think ahead and wonder if maybe Joe would participate someday. No one knew cattle or gave them better care than Joe—when he was able!

While parking the car and retracing the freshly poured sidewalk into the hospital, Olive forced her thoughts back to the present. Memories from the past and thoughts of the future were just too painful. The happy past brought too many depressing contrasts with the present, and the future held too many frightening unknowns.

CHAPTER 13

HOPE GONE

Olive sat straight up at the sound of the telephone ringing, her heart thumping. A call in the middle of the night must mean trouble. The only question in Olive's mind as she stumbled toward her bedroom door was whether the call was coming from home or the hospital. A stirring in the room across the hall told Olive that Oney or Alta had also been awakened by the telephone.

But Olive could not wait. She groped through the dark to the kitchen and grabbed for the receiver. "Hello!" she nearly shouted, and then listened intently. It was Abbey Delaney, an acquaintance from several years back. As nurse in the ward where Joe had now spent several weeks, she had stood by Olive during some very dark days, and they had become friends. "I see," she said. "I'll be there right away. Thanks, Abbey."

Oney, who had entered the kitchen on Olive's heels, whispered, "Bad news, I guess."

Olive turned toward him and said, "Yes. That was Abbey, the nurse at the hospital. She said Joe is slipping even more, and you know how bad he's been. I need to get to the hospital, Oney."

"Go get dressed, and I'll catch Jake," Oney said. Jake was the man who boarded in their home. "He'll be driving in any minute from work. He'll be glad to take you. I'll bring Alta down later. We'll sit with you."

Despite efforts during the past two months not to think about the future, Olive felt that she had already experienced the events that followed that phone call. She dressed, got in the car, and rode the familiar route to the hospital in a numb stupor. Then she made her way up the sidewalk, slid through the halls, and entered Joe's room.

As she pushed the door open, the shallow, rapid breathing of Joe's emaciated body was the only sound she heard. She approached the bed. Abbey turned and grasped Olive's hand. Olive searched for some last ray of hope in Abbey Delaney's face, even though her voice on the phone had not contained any hint of optimism at all.

CHAPTER 14

NO ANSWERS

The sound of footsteps behind her chair brought Olive quickly from the half nap she had taken. She glanced at the clock to discover that morning had come and felt Alta's hand resting lightly on her shoulder.

"How is he?" Alta whispered.

"There's very little life left in him. He's fought so long and so hard. It will take a miracle, Alt."

"Oney's gone back to sit with the boys. He asked me to call him with a report. I'll do that. Then I'll be back to sit with you. Can I bring you some coffee?"

"I'd appreciate it."

Doctor Williams met Alta as she left. "Good morning." He walked directly to Joe's bed.

"I don't understand, Doctor. The biggest, strongest one in the family—the one who's never been sick—why can't he shake this?" Olive asked, searching for an answer that could help her make sense of Joe's condition.

"I don't understand it either," the doctor replied. "I've seen this before, though. You've heard it said, 'The bigger they are, the harder they fall.' He seems to be resting easier, but he's failing fast. We've done all we can do. I'm sorry."

Olive rose from her chair, but with nothing more to say and no place to go, she just shook her head and allowed the tears to run down her cheeks. The question burning in her mind had become *what now* instead of *what if.*

Olive Jackson Bolser

Joseph Franklin Bolser

Homer, Fern, and Wesley

Homer and "Daddy Joe"

Aunt Lu

CHAPTER 15

FINAL HOUR

Eleven o'clock on Wednesday morning, November 28, 1928. The date and time were indelibly etched in Olive's memory as she and Alta watched Joe draw his last breath.

Numb and dazed, Olive turned to leave Joe's room for the last time and stood facing Joe's mother and brothers. Steadied on one side by Wellar and on the other by Carey, Joe's mother said, "Oney called. We came as soon as we could, but it's too late, isn't it?"

Olive nodded. She watched her mother-in-law walk to Joe's bedside and lean down over his body to accommodate her poor eyesight. As she took his hand, she raised her eyes and looked at Carey and Wellar. "This is such a shame," she said, her voice a little weaker and her eyes wet with tears.

As Carey and Wellar helped their mother to the chair, Olive's attention was drawn to the sound of footsteps at the door. The first feeling of anything that resembled relief and hope surfaced as she caught sight of her dear aunt Lu, her father's maiden sister. "He's gone," she whispered as the two embraced. "He's gone."

"We're here to help you through this," Aunt Lu said. "Come on. Uncle Ellsworth and Aunt Myrta are here too. Come with me now."

CHAPTER 16

BAD NEWS

"Do you need anything else, Olive? Do you want me to go into the house with you?" Uncle Ellsworth said as Olive stepped out of his car.

"No, you've done so much already—going to the funeral parlor to help me make arrangements. I have Abbey here with me. You go on home to Aunt Myrta," she replied.

Abbey followed closely behind Olive, up the narrow walk to the house where Olive's mother, Wesley, and Fern waited.

"Olive, she knows this isn't one of your regular afternoon visits," Abbey said when she saw her mother peering through the kitchen window and then moving toward the door. "Ellsworth bringing you home and my coming with you. She knows something is wrong."

Before Olive and Abbey reached the back door, she was on the porch. "Is Joe—"

Olive nodded. "We just left the funeral home."

"You poor girl." She pulled Olive close and guided her into the warm kitchen. "Here, sit down."

"Where are the children, Mom?"

"Wesley just woke up from his nap. I think Fern must have gone to check on him. I heard them talking and laughing just as you drove in. Homer's still at Sam's. Do you want to see them now, or would you rather rest a while?"

"I want to see them," Olive said. "Call Sam and ask him to bring Homer here. I don't know how much they'll understand, but I have to tell them. They're all I have now."

"I'll call Sam," Abbey said.

"I'll get Fern and Wesley if you're sure you're up to seeing them," her mom said. "I know they'll want to see you."

In no time, Fern had flown into the kitchen and onto her mother's lap. "Why are you late today?" she asked. "I've been waiting a long time."

At the sight of his mother, Wesley wiggled from his grandmother's arms and climbed up into Olive's lap too.

"You two look so good to me. It seems like a long time since I've been home," Olive said. "And this time, I don't have to leave you to go back to the hospital."

"Yeah!" Fern jumped from Olive's lap and clapped her hands.

"Yeah!" Wes said.

"You don't have to go see Daddy at the hospital anymore?" asked Fern.

"No, your daddy's gone."

"Gone? Where?" Fern asked.

"Well, he was so sick that the doctors and Nurse Abbey couldn't make him well. He died this morning, Fern. He won't be coming back."

"Oh," Fern replied as she pondered her mother's words. Then she turned to find the doll she had dropped when she first realized Olive was home.

CHAPTER 17

THANKSGIVING

*R*ing! Ring! Ring! Ring!
Olive roused herself from her fitful sleep, staring into the darkness and wondering if she had really heard the telephone. Or was she dreaming about the dreaded call that had summoned her to the hospital the night before?

Ring! Ring! Ring! Ring!

There it was again. The four rings had probably awakened every household on her party line. Olive flew through the house to the telephone on the kitchen wall. *What now? What could have happened now?* "Hello," she blurted into the receiver.

"Olive, this is Hap." In the stillness, the hired hand seemed to be shouting.

"Yes, Hap. What's wrong?" Her hand tightened around the receiver, dreading the answer and wondering what else could possibly go amiss.

"It's my daughter. She's been real sick, you know, and we called the doctor out here to see her tonight. She has diphtheria, and we're quarantined!"

"Quarantined?" Olive cried.

"I'm so sorry. I know how much you need help right now. I just don't know what I can do. I've been ordered to stay here, and you sure don't need diphtheria at your place. You think you can find help?"

"I don't know. I'll find someone, I hope. But don't worry— there's nothing you can do. Thanks for calling."

Olive forced from her thoughts all the memories of Joe's death and her plans for the funeral as she gathered strength to meet this new dilemma. She paced from one end of the kitchen to the other, and more questions than answers popped into her mind. *What will happen next? How much can I handle at one time? Who can I call out of bed to milk the cows?*

The calendar on the wall kept reminding her that this was Thanksgiving Day. It seemed to be mocking her. *What do I have to be thankful for?* She turned her back on the calendar and marched to the other end of the room.

Then she spotted the three pairs of shoes lined neatly against the wall. And though she could still not feel any sense of thankfulness in her present situation, she could not let herself give up.

Olive also knew who she should call right now. The one who had been there yesterday would help her today. Uncle Ellsworth Jones. Ringing the operator, Olive prepared herself for a long wait. Edna usually needed more time to make her way to her switchboard for those infrequent night or early-morning calls. But Olive was surprised by a quick reply to her ring. "Edna, I'm sorry to bother you so early, but I need to talk to my uncle, Ellsworth Jones. 3651."

"Are you all right?' Edna asked. "I heard about Joe."

"Well, I'm going to need help with my chores," Olive replied matter-of-factly.

"Okay, I'm ringing your uncle."

Olive waited and waited, knowing his aging body moved slowly in the morning. She hoped he didn't rush too quickly to the phone, but she yearned to hear his voice. Finally, a soft hello came through the phone, and she hurried to tell him who was calling.

"This is Olive, Uncle Ellsworth. I'm in a real bind. The hired hand is quarantined. How am I going to get the cows milked?"

"You are in a predicament!" he said. "We can work this out, though. I'll be over there in thirty minutes."

Still unsure of the solution to her problem, Olive sighed in relief as she put the receiver back on the wall.

CHAPTER 18

PAYING RESPECTS

"Come on, Brownie," Homer said. The dog had evidently managed to come into the house with one of the people who had come pay their respects. He seemed to realize that Joe's body lay in the box in the living room, and that to show his loyalty, he should lie underneath it. "You can't stay here. Too many people! Daddy Joe can't see you anyway. Come on!" Homer turned to walk toward the kitchen door and nearly bumped into a tall, thin man who offered his help.

"There he goes," the man murmured as his petted the dog and gave him a little push at the same time. "Looks like your dog misses your daddy like the rest of us do," he added.

Homer stared up into the man's face and nodded. "Did you know my daddy?"

"Yep! I'm Jack—one of the guys he played ball with on Sunday afternoons."

"Daddy told me about those games. Wish I could have gone to one!"

"We had some good times together. Your daddy wasn't just a good ballplayer, though. He was a fine man too. This crowd here for his visitation is a testimony to that. You've had a full house since I've been here."

Homer nodded and smiled at his new friend.

Across the room, Olive kept a watchful eye on Homer as she greeted the steady stream of visitors. Removing Brownie from under the casket was one of several actions that proved to Olive that Homer's word was true. She would never forget his reaction when she told Homer about his daddy's death. As she cried, he consoled her, "Don't worry, Mother. I'll take care of you."

He's going to have to grow up fast, thought Olive.

CHAPTER 19

FINAL RITES

"Are you all right, Olive?" Reverend Neal asked as the pallbearers carried the heavy casket from the hearse to the gravesite.

"Yes," she replied as he sat beside her. "Thank you for that beautiful service. It seems fitting that the one who married us should also preside over Joe's funeral."

"Well, it's a challenge to honor a man like Joe. We know he was something special, and—evidently—a lot of people agree. If it's all right with you, we're going to delay for few minutes here. The church was so full that not everyone was able to get inside. Several had to stand out in the rain or sit in their cars during the service. They tell me the procession from the church is two miles long. I'd like to give some of those folks time to get here before we say the final prayer."

"Yes, by all means, Reverend. Let's wait."

"Mother, what are we going to do now?" Fern sat on the chair to Olive's right.

"We're waiting for all the cars to get here," Olive whispered.

"I'm wet, and I'm getting cold!" Fern said.

"Here," Abbey said, reaching for Fern. "Come sit on my lap. We'll keep each other warm. See Homer over there by Grandma Jackson? See what a big boy he is? So quiet, so still. Let's sit here by him for a while. Then we'll be going home. Come on."

"Look there," Fern called as she jumped onto Abbey's lap.

"There's Grandma Bolser and Uncle Oney. He's the one Mother stayed with when Daddy was in the hospital. Look, Homer. There's Uncle Sam and Aunt Marie. That's who you stayed with. I know lots of people here, but I don't know everybody. Who's that? And that?"

"Sh," Abbey whispered in Fern's ear. "Turn around here and be quiet for just a little while."

"Let us pray," Reverend Neal said in a loud voice.

The crowd of heads bowed.

"We commend the soul of this loved one to you, our God, the One who knows and sees beyond what we can fathom. We ask your divine protection and guidance for those who depended on this man the most. We take comfort in your words, 'The Lord is my shepherd.'"

CHAPTER 20

HELPING HANDS

"Eat another pancake before we start the washing," Olive's mother said.

"No, I'm not that hungry," she answered as she pushed her chair from the table.

"You should be! Doing the barn work and all your normal housework besides!"

"Only for a couple more weeks, though. I scheduled the auction yesterday, December 20. With Aunt Lu and Uncle Ellsworth's help, I'll keep the milking going. The only cow I can't handle is Bessie, and Glenn from down the road said he would come milk her for the next few weeks. But I'm still worried about how—"

"What do I hear?" Olive's mother said.

"There's a whole army of men out in the barnyard!" Homer said as he burst into the kitchen. "The only one I've ever seen before is Jack."

"Jack? Who's Jack? What could they want?" Olive grabbed her coat and flew out the door to meet the men walking toward the house. "Can I help you?" Olive searched their faces for clues about what they might want.

"No, ma'am. We're here to help you," the man in front said. "We've come to husk and crib Joe's corn. Is it all right with you if we get started?"

"Well, yes. Sure. Please. I mean thank you! That's just what I've been concerned about. Several of you were here for Joe's viewing, weren't you?"

"Yes, ma'am."

"Just call me Olive. I'll try to learn some of your names too. I think I've even forgotten those I met that night you were here."

"Is that the corncrib you want us to put the corn in?" One of the men pointed across the barnyard.

"Yes," Olive replied. "I'll send my son out. He's little, but he was always in his daddy's hip pocket. He can answer any questions you have. Thank you," she said as she turned and ran back to the house.

"Oh, Olive," one of the men called timidly. "Don't go to any trouble fixing us dinner. We brought sack lunches."

"How will I ever repay you?" she called back.

The man had turned and seemed not to hear her question.

"Mom, you'll never guess what's happening right now!" Olive exclaimed as she entered the kitchen and hurriedly hung her coat on its hook. "They've come to take care of the corn! The one huge task left before the auction! I was really worried about this."

"Who are they?" Homer and his grandmother asked at the same time.

"Joe's friends. I think he knew most of them from playing baseball. I remember several of them being here for Joe's viewing. Homer, go on out there and do what you can to help. And don't get in their way. Mom, you and I are going to have to fix a big batch of doughnuts and coffee."

CHAPTER 21

UNWELCOME SURPRISE

Olive stepped through the doorway of Aunt Lu's house. She surveyed the room and said, "Ten years and some unusual tenants have made a big difference in this house. It's going to take a lot of work, but I'm so glad it's here for us. I just don't know what we'd have done without you and your old house."

"This place brings back a lot of memories, doesn't it?" Aunt Lu said as she walked from the back door through the house to the front door that faced Main Street. "You remember my milliner's shop, don't you? Those were the days when every lady, even in this little town, needed several fashionable hats! This was a busy place for about ten years."

"Those were good days," Olive said. "I loved visiting you and Grandma here. Even after Grandma died and the hat business fell off, I liked spending weekends with you while the boarders were gone."

"Yes, but that was a lonely time for me. That's why I rented this house and came to live with your folks for a while. I debated some about whether to keep the house. I knew I'd never marry. Grandma kept me single too long for that." She sighed. "I'm certainly glad I have it now. I never dreamed I'd ever be moving back in. And not with you and your family!"

"What's that smell?" Olive asked. "It was really strong as we walked through that middle room."

Aunt Lu and Olive retraced their steps, following their noses to a closet in the corner of the other room. Aunt Lu opened the closet door, and they both turned to the opposite wall, rushing for the window and some fresh air!

"I've never smelled anything so awful!" Aunt Lu said. "I was afraid of this though," she added, wrinkling her brow and staring at the closet.

"Why? What made this mess?" Olive inched a little closer, peering in the closet.

"Well, people have told me stories about these last tenants," Aunt Lu said. "One rumor was that they had a pet monkey. I wondered where they would keep it, and I think we may have just discovered it."

"Our cow stable smelled better than that closet!"

"I'm glad it's January instead of a hot day in July!" Aunt Lu added.

"I thought the dirty walls and gummy floors were a challenge," Olive responded. "This closet is a nightmare! How do we start to clean it?"

"With buckets and mops and soap and water and rags and scrub brushes, I guess," Aunt Lu said. "Let's leave the window open. We'll be working too hard to get cold, and we'll need the fresh air!"

CHAPTER 22

JOB SEARCH

"Ladies and gentlemen," the short, stocky man on the steps said. "We're going to ask you to form two lines today." Every cold ear was tuned to catch the words being spoken. "Please move over here to my left and form a separate line if you're the breadwinner for your family. We ask that the rest of you stay where you are for now."

As Olive's numb feet moved quickly to the new line, her heart was lifted with renewed hope. *Maybe as a "breadwinner," I'll have an edge on getting a job.* When she joined the breadwinner line, she noted that almost half the other people moved with her. *I'm still vying with at least twenty other people. Please let me get a job.*

A year or two ago, jobs were plentiful and easy to come by, but recent stories about overproduction and falling prices seemed to be more than baseless rumors. Now, in the winter of 1929, unemployment had become a real concern.

Eager eyes focused on the drab green door leading to the Stearns and Foster employment office. Olive, like most of the others, had stood here two or three times before, waiting for hours only to be disappointed with the announcement, "No more hiring today!"

Snow began to fall, and the hushed voices of those in line were barely audible as the stamping of feet from nervousness and cold increased. Then, after what seemed like an eternity, the door opened again. Two people at the front of the breadwinner line were admitted into the employment office. A ripple of conversation passed through the crowd, mostly questions posed to one another:

"Were there just two?" an exasperated man a few feet in front of Olive asked.

"They came from the breadwinners line, didn't they?" someone else asked. "Do you suppose they'll be back out?"

"Maybe they'll hire all of us. Two at a time!" An optimist chuckled at his own remark.

The stocky man reappeared and quickly pulled in five more people from near the front of the line, coming close to Olive. This time, questions were shouted loud enough for the man at the door to hear.

"Are you hiring a lot today?"

"How many do you need?"

"Will you interview us all?"

"Give us all a chance?"

The man turned quickly and herded his group of five through the door without looking at or responding to the crowd. *Maybe I'll be next*, Olive thought. *Please, God, let me be next!*

The snow stopped and started again, accumulating in some spots. Minutes, then an hour passed, toes and fingers numbing, hopes dying.

The man reappeared, looking tired and worried. "No more hiring today. We expect that we will not need any new employees for several months." He turned, shook his head, and quickly retreated inside the door.

CHAPTER 23

FAMILY MEETING

"Go on now and don't worry about me and the kids," Aunt Lu said. "I'm feeling pretty good today, and the kids are fed and happy. Besides, I'll bet you won't be there long."

"I don't know," Olive replied. "I just don't know what to think. Wellar's not much of a talker and was especially quiet the other day."

"I noticed that," Aunt Lu said. "What did he say? They wanted you out to his house for a meeting? Is that how he put it?"

"Yes, and not to bring the kids. I'm really wondering about this. I guess I just don't know Joe's mother and brothers as well as my family. I can't figure this out."

"Oh, go on. They probably just want to know how they can help," Aunt Lu said.

"Probably. But to call a *meeting*? That makes me wonder. I guess I'll never find out standing here. Are you sure you're feeling all right?"

"Yes, yes. I'm fine. Now go on! You can tell me all about it when you get back."

The short drive from West Chester to the Bolser farm gave Olive little time to draw any new conclusions about the purpose of the meeting. Joe's five older brothers and his parents had always been friendly and supportive toward Joe and his family, but the ties were not as close as those in Olive's family. Olive had appreciated their help during Joe's illness, but she had naturally leaned most on her own family while trying to recover from Joe's death and caring for her children.

Wellar, the second oldest of the six sons, ran the Bolser farm now since he was unmarried at the time of his father's death two years ago. Mary Bolser was able to live in her home after being widowed. She had come to depend more and more on Wellar to run the farm and care for her.

"Come in, Olive." Wellar met her at the back door. "Let me take your coat. The others are sitting in the dining room."

"Am I late? Is everyone waiting on me?" Olive asked.

"Oh, no. The others came early. We've been visiting. We don't seem to get together much."

Why now? Olive wondered.

"Hello, Olive." Marie said.

"Good to see you," Olive replied, remembering the good care Marie and Sam had given Homer while Joe was in the hospital.

Alta crossed the room to greet her. "How are you, Olive?"

"I'm going to make it," she replied. She once again felt grateful for the room and board Alta and Oney had provided during Joe's illness.

"Have a seat, Olive," Mother Bolser said. "I think we have enough chairs for everyone."

The room was silent for a few awkward seconds.

Oney cleared his throat, looked around the room, and said "We're worried about you, Olive, and about your kids. We don't see how you're going to make it. That three thousand dollars you got from the auction won't last long. You can't get through this without help. So we have talked it over and have come up with a plan."

Olive stared at him, her heart pounding and her stomach turning flips. She was extremely anxious about their "plan."

Looking around the room, Oney continued. "We thought it best if Sam and Marie kept Homer. You know they all did so well together while Joe was sick. And Alta and I could take Fern. You could probably keep Wesley and make it—at least try it."

All eyes were glued on Olive. In shock, she sat silently for a few long seconds. The silence was deafening. Suddenly Olive felt a rush of blood to her face, her hands shook, and a shot of adrenaline sent her to her feet. Words flew from her mouth. "Come hell or high water, I will keep my children and raise them my way!"

No one moved but Olive. She grabbed her coat and marched out of the house to her automobile in the barnyard. Working frantically to get the engine started, she was unaware that Wellar had followed her. As she hopped into the driver's seat, he said, "Olive, you did just right. I didn't know before how you'd react, but I do understand how you must feel. You keep those kids. Joe would want you all together. I don't have much cash, but if there's anything I can do to help, you just let me know."

"Thanks, Wellar. That's just what I intend to do. I appreciate your understanding and concern." Olive drove home more determined than ever to find work and support her family.

CHAPTER 24

MEN'S WORK

"Is there a second to the motion?"

"I'll second the motion."

"All in favor, say aye. Opposed?"

Olive shuffled her feet and sat up a little straighter. *Surely my chance will come soon,* she thought. For forty-five minutes, the school board had dealt with detail after detail, denying Olive the opportunity to put her plan into action.

"Well, before we go on to new business," Mr. Eiler drawled, "we need to take a look here at the end of the school year at our buses. I'm not aware of any need for change, but I did ask Mr. Bristol to attend this meeting and report on any issues he has concerning the operation of his bus service to our school."

All eyes darted to Mr. Bristol, owner of the two $750 motorized buses that had replaced the horse-drawn buses of a few years ago. Before he could speak, Olive was on her feet. "Mr. Chairman, excuse me, but I'm here tonight to apply in person for a bus driver's job—if you need one."

All eyes were on Olive. No one spoke for a few long seconds.

Olive added, "Most of you know how much I need a job right now. I'm well qualified. I've been driving since I was fifteen. I'd do a good job."

Mr. Eiler fumbled for words and looked at Mr. Bristol for input. "I'm not at all sure we need another bus driver, and besides—"

"But I was just about to propose that," Mr. Bristol said. "I do need a driver for one route. I could give the shorter of two routes to Mrs. Bolser. I've talked to her, and I think she could handle it well."

The five board members looked at each other, but no one was sure of what to say.

"That eight dollars a day would go a long way toward supporting my family," Olive said.

Mr. Beekley said, "But has anyone ever heard of a lady bus driver? I just don't think it's ever done around here!"

"I say let's try it." Mr. Aufranc was the youngest member of the board. "Not many ladies in this town drive, but those who do are just as good as the men."

"I agree," Mr. Davis said. "She needs a job, and we need a bus driver."

"I don't know." Mr. Eiler sighed and shook his head. "Some parents won't let their youngsters ride with a lady bus driver. They will figure she can't handle it. This is just unheard of, you know, but let's put it to a vote. Those in favor of hiring Mrs. Bolser to take the short route, say aye."

Mr. Aufranc and Mr. Davis loudly said, "Aye!"

"Opposed?" Mr. Eiler called.

"Aye!" the other two responded.

"I'm sorry, Mrs. Bolser," Mr. Eiler said. "It's up to me to break the tie, and I truly feel that it would be unwise to hire a lady to drive one of our buses."

CHAPTER 25

UNEXPECTED GIFT

Carrying water and kindling were demanding jobs for a six-year-old boy, but when chores were finished, Homer always had plenty of energy left for play with his new friends.

"Two hours until suppertime," Olive called as Homer pushed open the screen door. "Don't stray too far."

"Okay," Homer yelled over his shoulder. *Plenty of time to get to the creek and back,* he thought as he grabbed the old rusty tire rim he'd set next to the house. He liked rolling it along, guiding it with a stick on his journeys to the creek or the post office.

Concentrating on the path of his wobbling tire rim, Homer was taken by surprise when he heard his name. Through the screen door of the house next to his, the voice said, "Homer, can you run an errand for me?" Homer caught the metal rim and dragged it closer to Edna Schick's house. The creek and rim could wait. An errand for this neighbor always meant a few pennies for his pocket, and today, he had a special purpose for his pennies.

"Take this down to Jack." Mrs. Schick handed Homer a bag. "And then stop at the post office and get my mail. Can you do that for me today?"

"Just a minute." Homer set the rim against the house and ran to the open door.

"Here." Mrs. Schick handed him the bag to be delivered to her husband at his barber shop. "Now don't forget my mail!"

"Okay." Homer raced down the street, reaching the red-and-white barber pole in a matter of seconds.

"Hi, there!" Jack was snipping at his customer's beard with his sharp silver scissors. "Something for me?"

"Yeah, Mrs. Schick asked me to bring this to you on my way to get your mail."

"All right. Thanks, son. Just lay it on the counter over there."

"Bye." Homer headed for the door and stepped out into the bright sunshine. Squinting, he looked both ways for cars and crossed the street to the house that served as the post office.

"Back again?" asked Mary Cramer. "You're a busy boy, aren't you?"

"This time I need Mrs. Schick's mail," Homer replied. He had fetched the mail for his mother and Aunt Lu only a couple of hours earlier.

"Here it is." Mary gathered a few envelopes from one of the slots in the wall. "I believe you must be a good mailman."

"Thanks," Homer said, and he set off to Mrs. Schick's house. One knock brought her to the door.

"Thank you," Mrs. Schick said as she placed a shiny nickel in his hand. "Here's a little extra for such a fast delivery."

Homer had one more errand before he could go back to his tire rim and his trip to the creek. The errand was made possible by the shiny new nickel in his hand.

The bell on the door of the dry goods store jingled as it closed behind him. Footsteps behind the curtain told Homer that Mr. Hoerst was coming to help him. Homer blinked, adjusting to the dim light. Through glass cases set on a wooden counter, he gazed at jewelry, hatpins, and scarves.

"Can I help you?" Mr. Hoerst asked.

"I have a nickel," Homer said. "And I need to buy my mother a birthday present."

"Let's see." Mr. Hoerst scanned the articles on display. "How about this handkerchief? See the little purple flowers embroidered on each corner? Looks like a good gift to me!"

"Purple is Mother's favorite color. That's what I want," Homer stated.

Mr. Hoerst tucked it neatly into a small paper bag. "That's five cents."

Homer handed Mr. Hoerst the nickel.

Mr. Hoerst passed the bag over the counter to Homer. "Thank you—and wish your mother a happy birthday for me."

"Okay," Homer replied, anxious to get home and bring a smile to Mother's worried face.

Olive peeked into the kitchen when she heard the screen door slam.

"For your birthday," Homer said as he handed her the bag.

Olive opened the bag and pulled out the beautifully stitched handkerchief.

Homer's wish came true. Her smile and tears of joy told him it was a happy birthday in spite of their troubles.

CHAPTER 26

MAKING ENDS MEET

The sweater felt good in the coolness of the early morning. And the warm coffee cake tasted good. Grabbing one more bite as Mother hurried him out the door, Homer savored its flavor. The aroma had tempted him as he awoke, and it reminded him that it was Saturday morning—time to make his deliveries.

After several months of making his biweekly deliveries, Homer had memorized his route. To the south end of town, he would pull his green metal wagon and begin his day. The cakes, nestled tightly into a wooden crate and covered with an old tablecloth, were delivered to his regular customers early every Wednesday and Saturday mornings.

"Two for Edna Schick, two for Maude Jones, and one for Julia Conrad," Homer said as he pointed to the cakes.

"Then two more for Mary Cramer at the post office," Olive reminded him as she fit two more cakes in the box. "Hurry back," she called as she returned to get the cakes ready for the north end of town. It usually took Homer about thirty minutes to collect a quarter for each cake and return to finish the job with cakes she had in the oven.

The day had been a long one for Olive. She had risen at three to start baking. She squeezed the metal clamp tightly around the top of the twenty-five-pound bag of flour and pushed it to the side. Olive drove out to Fred DeBord's store every week or two to replenish her supply. She was so grateful that Fred helped her by selling the flour to her at cost. Olive continued to tidy the kitchen and watch the cakes while she waited for Homer's return.

"That was a quick trip! Was everyone home?" she asked as he bounded into the kitchen.

"Yeah, and here are the seven quarters—and an extra nickel Miss Conrad gave to me."

"Good job! Better get these delivered now." Olive removed the cakes from the oven. "Be careful. These are really hot." One by one, she lifted them from the rack in the oven and carried them out to the crate in the wagon. "Don't forget the new customer next to Grace Thompson's. And Mrs. Peele wants two this week instead of one."

"I'll be back in a few minutes." Homer stuffed another bite of his cake into his mouth.

CHAPTER 27

CHRISTMAS

December 25, 1929, was a cold, dark day. A year after the funeral. A year after the auction. Olive, Homer, Fern, and Wesley had survived as a family for one long year without Joe.

How long can coffee cakes and occasional housecleaning jobs keep us going? The happy, secure Christmases of just a couple of years ago seemed like a dream as Olive rose from the cold, lonely bed. *I wish there were some way I could make this day special.* She quickly dressed in her warmest clothes.

Slowly, quietly so as not to wake the children, Olive descended the stairs and was startled to hear a loud rap at the door. Jerking into a near run, she headed for the kitchen.

"Merry Christmas!" her father's cousin called through the back door.

"Roy Bowen? What are you doing here? Haven't seen you for months—and here you are on my back step on Christmas morning!"

"Been thinking about you a lot, Olive. Know it can't be easy for you with three little ones and Joe gone. Could you use some extra food for Christmas?"

"My budget has been awful slim, Roy. It has been a rough year for us."

"Look in this box then. Maybe this will help." Roy set a large box on the table with a thump. Olive peered into the box and smiled gratefully. There were several cuts of pork, half a shoulder, fresh sausage, bacon, spareribs, and lard. She also found two chickens and four dozen eggs.

"You're an answer to my prayers, Roy! Thank you—and merry Christmas!"

Chapter 28

New Hope

"It's good to see you smiling again," Aunt Lu said as Olive finished the last bite of the fried cornmeal mush the two shared on cold winter mornings.

"I think we're going to make it now, Aunt Lu. They tell me that the county pension fund has been built up again, and I'm eligible for a ten-dollar-a-month payment. Also, the janitor at the school needs help. I talked to him yesterday, and he says I can start to work for him next week. That will bring in ten dollars a week! I just worry about leaving you here watching Wesley and Fern while Homer and I are working at the school in the afternoons and evenings."

"We will be just fine. I like to think I can still be of some help."

"We need more wood in the stove. I'm chilly." Olive grabbed another handful of kindling. The fire blazed brighter as she threw it into the stove, and she felt a sudden surge of heat. As she turned to clear the table, she said, "We're going to make it now, Aunt Lu. I just know we are going to make it!"

Epilogue

Olive Jackson Bolser married George W. Hoffman in 1932. Together, they farmed and raised Olive's three children. They celebrated their fiftieth anniversary just prior to George's death at the age of eighty-five. Olive was ninety-four when she died in 1997.